Buying a Business

The quick and easy guide for small business owners

Mike Knight

MBA FCIM

3P Publishing

C E C, London Road Corby

NN17 5EU

ISBN: 978-1-913740-32-0

Cover design: James Mossop

Contents

In this book, we'll look at the following 10 steps involved in purchasing a company.

Preface

Having run my own business since 1998, I first become involved in helping other business owners sell their businesses in 2018, with my first business sale being of a managed service provider (MSP), where the owner wanted to leave the UK and travel to America to join the circus; life can sometimes be stranger than fiction.

After helping more and more business owners sell up and retire or move on to other things, it occurred to me that many business owners could achieve growth by acquisition (with all the benefits this brings), yet for various reasons it remains a blind spot for many entrepreneurs, hence putting together this straightforward guide. I hope you find it useful.

Michael Knight
MBA FCIM

1
Why Buy a Business, Anyway?

Reasons to Grow Your Business by Acquiring Another Business

- Faster growth. By buying another business (in the same industry), you can increase the growth of your business much faster than could be achieved by organic growth and/or marketing alone.

- Opportunity for attractive RoI. If you purchase a business that has great potential but is struggling and/or undervalued, you can pick up a bargain, thereby acquiring clients at a fraction of the usual acquisition costs.

- Access to motivated sellers. Baby boomers looking to retire are now proving to be a good source of motivated sellers and the sheer amount of them can provide attractive oversupply prices.

- Financial leverage. You can leverage asset(s) in the target business to acquire commercial finance to purchase the company and therefore acquire significantly more customers than you could otherwise afford alone.

- Vendor finance. If the business owner is prepared to sell their business to you, this means it will not affect your credit rating, plus you can likely get better terms and ultimately better ROI.

- Economies of scale - purchasing power. A larger company with more turnover of supplies can very often command better prices and terms, thereby rationalising overhead.

- Access to clients. You can have access to their clients and dispense with a lot of their fixed costs. By de-duplicating cost centres such as marketing, admin, office-rent, rates etc., you can essentially have access to the "good stuff" and simply cut out the expensive stuff by leveraging existing resources an deduplication of cost centres.

- Access to different or better products, services and skills. Your target business may have some key resources that your business lacks. You can diversify and potentially have access to products and services more cheaply than developing them yourself.

- Access to better, higher profile clients. Your target business may have some clients which may provide a large revenue or which would be strategically important for you, not least of which may simply be leveraging their 'name-dropping' value.

- Access broader client base. The business you are considering purchasing may have clients in areas where you need to expand and/or have access to distribution channels you may not currently exploit. In turn, this can increase your market share, penetration and visibility.

- Reduced competition. When you literally buy-out your competition, you may be able to increase prices and profits directly.

- Personal development and satisfaction. Buying another business elevates you above the vast majority of SMEs that never acquire another one and means you'll be operating at a different level to the typical 'owner-operator'. You now have a business owner mentality (i.e. working on the businesses) rather than an employee mentality (i.e. working in the businesses).

- Public Relations (PR). Half of business is about trust and confidence. Demonstrating to the world that you've acquired another business radiates confidence, ambition and acumen.

- Reduced risk. Owning more than one business means that if one business fails for some reason, you can still have income from another. Creating a start-up has a greater than average chance of failing within five years, whilst a (correctly purchased) business acquired has a greater than average chance of still trading after five years.

All of the above benefits assume that you're looking to buy another company in the same industry as the one you currently operate in, i.e. a company that is similar to yours primarily to expand your client base.

Whilst it's outside the scope of this book, there are other strategic reasons that businesses buy other businesses which happen to be outside their core operations. It's a well-known fact that a frightening proportion of start-ups fail before their first birthday and if they've made it to their fifth birthday, they can consider themselves lucky.

So, if a start-up survives the first few years, it's significantly more likely to succeed by virtue of having overcome the particularly taxing challenges at inception. A bit like being born in the middle ages ... you were a lot more likely to survive to adulthood if you've survived past being a toddler!

For this reason, if you're looking to grow your business by investing into (untested) new technologies or disruptive procedures for example, which are currently outside your core competency or areas of activity, it can make sense to avoid many of the pitfalls of in-house development (or acquisition of a risky start-up) by acquiring a bolt-on new(ish) businesses that has survived (say) the first two or three years. So, if you're looking to acquire another, complementary business (but not a raw start-up) for those reasons, then the main benefits can be:

- Instant income. As well as increased security through diversification, your business can enjoy immediate, increased cash-flow as well, depending on how the up-front purchase costs are structured and whether that business is profitable or distressed.

- Established brand. Customers, suppliers, investors and even staff can be wary about dealing with new, unknown business propositions. Acquiring an established brand (and goodwill) can help overcome this and also provides an ...

- Established network of contacts. That little black book that worth its weight in gold.

- Diversification. It can pay to have a mixed portfolio of product or service offerings in your areas of operations.

- Vertical integration. For example, buying yourself out of supplier "lock-in". If you have few suppliers for an essential part of your business, it can be more profitable to bring them in house.

- Tried and tested systems and procedures. Rather than having to reinvent the wheel for developing a new product or service, purchasing an established (proven) business can eliminate these obstacles.

- Trained staff in place. A good deal of overhead in terms of time, training costs, mistakes and general sweat and tears can be avoided when trained staff are already in place and who can run the business smoothly (ideally without you) and be enlisted to grow the business as well, when they're suitably re-energised and motivated by new leadership.

2
Potential Pitfalls

It would be remiss to suggest that growing by acquisition is a simple panacea for all challenges incurred when growing a business. There are risks involved in any venture, no matter how well planned and executed. Things can go wrong, sometimes badly. It's worth considering the risks:

⇨ Time

At the very least, even if all your ventures are largely problem free, there will be a significant overhead in terms of time sacrificed. Unlike money, time cannot be replenished and once it's gone, it's gone. Every hour spent on a potential purchase incurs the opportunity-cost of time that could be invested improving an existing, profitable enterprise. When looking for opportunities, it's likely you'll have to 'kiss a lot of frogs' before the ideal one comes along.

Even when the right one comes along, the sale often doesn't go through, for various reasons beyond your control. If a lot of time has already been clocked up whilst undergoing all the various checks and due-diligence, this can have a motivational impact as well.

Furthermore, even after a successful purchase, a lot of time will be required to complete the deal and implement the requisite changes to the new acquisition.

⇨ Money

Again (in terms of money), there is an opportunity cost even if a transaction is successful, at least initially until cash-flow is forthcoming. If the purchase doesn't go ahead, there will be some losses incurred as a result of costs associated with due diligence, professional fees etc. If the purchase does go ahead - and the new business acquisition fails - you could lose your entire investment.

Furthermore, if there are personal guarantees involved, you could lose a lot more.

⇨ **Liabilities**

When someone acquires a new business (a share purchase), they are also acquiring that company's liabilities. Tax liabilities, creditor liabilities, legal liabilities ... there are a lot of responsibilities. It is possible to purchase just the assets rather than the company itself, but even then one must be careful that the assets aren't already incumbered with debt.

If a customer, supplier, staff member or member of the general public is suing a business, they don't care that the owners are new and weren't there at the time of any issue(s) that arose, they will simply be seeking compensation from the business and potentially the owners as well.

It is not unknown for the new owners of a business to go to prison for issues caused by the previous owners.

⇨ **People**

Where people are involved, things can easily go wrong or turn sour. The vendor may simply copy all your ideas and not sell your business. They may sell last minute to a competitor. The staff may decide they want to leave (potentially to a competitor). The vendor may not fulfil crucial parts of their contract, making operating the business almost impossible, yet difficult to sue. In short, people are a funny lot and they don't always play ball. The reality is that a large percentage of acquisitions fail. But for entrepreneurs, it's all part of the challenge and cut-and-thrust of business in general. It's what makes the successes so much more exhilarating, beyond the financial rewards of course!

3
The Type of Business You Want

Opportunities abound and so clarity and focus are essential, otherwise wasted efforts or overwhelm (and a consequent lack of action) are likely.

When it comes to growing a business portfolio rather than just maintaining a lifestyle choice, some B2B business industries are simply better than others to be in. In the SME arena, it's easier to consolidate and scale (say) an IT Support business, accountancy practice or training provider for example, where systems and processes can be replicated, than (say) a meat processing plant. Think in terms of simplicity around systems, scaling and/ or duplication.

Depending on your circumstances, your criteria will change, although the following bullet points are largely useful rules of thumb when selecting a (type of) business to acquire. For the remainder of this text, we'll assuming we're talking about an acquisition for growth in the same industry for the same clients, rather than a strategic purchase (e.g. purchasing a supplier).

This being the case, a target company should ideally have the following criteria ...

- The business should own an asset. When the business has an asset of some kind, it's likely you can get finance for it, therefore you don't have to risk (or tie up) your own capital. Assets that you can finance against include property, stock, equipment, trade debtors and future cash-flow. Future cash-flow will ideally be protected with *contracts*. Indeed, the contracts are often the primary reasons a purchaser is interested in the business, otherwise the clients could walk away as soon as the business is sold.

- Recurring revenue. To reiterate, 'cash is king' and consequently, if your clients pay you monthly (held in a contract), ideally via direct debit, then you are better equipped to weather storms, leverage the cash-flow for finance and increase prices and sales-throughput with less resistance.

- Premium pricing. Businesses that rely on price alone to differentiate (i.e. commoditised) typically need to get big to be profitable, which can carries its own risk and may be outside the reach or requirements of many SME owners. However, those businesses that tend to carry good profit margins are likely lend themselves to easier financing. Wider margins provide a 'safety buffer'.

New, Old ... and Franchises

There are three main types of business opportunities to consider when seeking to expand by acquisition, namely franchises, start-ups and existing businesses.

Given that franchises are mostly strictly controlled in terms of operations and marketing etc., we will not be considering them here.

Start-ups do not enjoy many of the benefits that an established business has, such as proven products/services, systems, processes, cash-flow and - crucially - clients. For these reasons alone, start-ups are also discounted here.

For this study, we are only looking for established businesses to acquire (ideally at least a couple of years old that have proven themselves to be potentially viable, even if they are distressed), that will add the most value to our portfolio, for the least amount of risk and cost.Typically, when people look to acquire another business, it will be to create some kind of synergy with existing staff, clients, suppliers or other enterprises that the buyer owns.

- Same industry, same clients. These businesses are in exactly the same industry as yours because you're looking to grow by acquisition as part of your growth strategy (which is what we're discussing in this text). Consolidation of smaller business can prove very profitable.

- Complementary industry, same clients. These are ones that complement your existing company. This company sells different products or services to your existing company but has access to the same types of customers that you want. e.g., IT support and telephony are two different services but can share the same clients - or at least a significant proportion of them.

- Different industry, different clients. These are in a different industry but may have a benefit to the rest of your portfolio. e.g., an IT support company might buy a software company for strategic reasons as it uses a particular CRM or platform that all its other companies can use. Or it might be more cost effective to buy a supplier than simply keep paying a premium to that supplier for goods or services.

The State Of Play

Once you've decided the kind of business you want, you'll ideally have a strategy for the *state* of the business you're looking to buy. Are you looking for a highly profitable one that you can simply bolt-on to your existing business/portfolio, or are you looking for one that's underperforming (and likely in distress and thus cheap) so that you can fix the problems and generate profits later?

With a *profitable* business you can expect instant cash-flow but you're likely to pay a premium for it. With a *distressed* business, you can probably negotiate great terms but will need to invest time/money fixing it.

Obviously, you'll want to avoid paying a premium for a so-called profitable business only to find that it is distressed in some way and conversely you'd not wish to keep investing time and money in a distressed business to discover that it is beyond repair.

If you can find a distressed business and turn it around easily, or find a profitable business that that you can acquire for cheaply/ no money down then you can make your cash very quickly.

Distressed Businesses

A profitable business *makes money*. It's easy to see. What's a lot harder to see is a business that appears profitable but which has underlying problems that are either current, contingent or imminent. A business can be distressed for any number of reasons.

Naturally, the easiest way to tell if the business is distressed is if *the owner tells you*. Hopefully, the owner will be transparent about the issues involved and you can make a judgement call - up front - about whether or not (in principle) you can fix the business and profitably turn it around.

Factors causing businesses to become distressed are numerous although some common causes are listed below. In general, the reasons are either attributed to issues that have affected the business directly or issues that have affected the owner (or a key member of staff) such as bereavement, illness (including depression/ alcoholism or other disorders), divorce, family problems etc. Issues that involve the business owner directly (as above) may well mean that the business could simply become healthy and viable gain when sufficient time running it properly is re-established.

Issues directly affecting the business can include:

- Over-competition.

- Under-pricing.

- Undertrained / poorly performing staff.

- Incompetence / indifference.

- Management or staffing costs too high.

- Overburdened with debt.

- Increase in expenses.

- Loss of income.

- Loss of a key customer/supplier/staff member.

- General industry downturn.

- Unexpected event such as litigation/tax liability/security hack etc.

Some of these issues can be fixed relatively (e.g., under-pricing or staffing costs) whilst other ones may prove insurmountable (e.g., loss of key contracts, industry downturn or litigation) and you're either better off walking away or considering purchasing the assets only.

⇨ **Signs that a business is in distress**

Remember, the business may well be distressed - or about to become distressed - without the owner telling you. If, acting on the information you've been given so far, you decide to move forwards from this stage towards *making an offer* (whilst unknown to you there are significant underlying issues), then hopefully these problems will be picked up in the *due diligence stage* - outlined later in this text.

Who is Going to be Managing the Company?

Will you be managing it? Does the company manage itself? (Note, smaller businesses are often owner-operators and therefore the person selling the business may be key to its operations. It's one of the biggest challenges when trying to expand if you're too involved in the day to day running of your business).

Will your existing company manage the acquired business? Will you hire someone to manage the business or will you outsource everything to an outside agency (e.g. an outsourced HR company).

Again, for the purpose of this text, I'm assuming that you're simply looking to grow your customer base and add the new business to your existing business to grow by acquisition. However, you have other choices of what to do for your newly acquired business:

- Manage it 'as is' and simply bolt-it on to your existing business.

- "Fix it" ... then manage it 'as is' and simply bolt-it on to your existing business.

- Sell it, after adding value (i.e. 'flip' it).

- A combination: i.e. retain part of the business (or assets) and sell the rest.

4
Fixing

In order to make your acquisition work, at some point you'll need to either add value to it, cut costs ... or both. If you managed to acquire the company at below market value, you've created wealth straight away. Even if that is the case, it is still important to look for ways to either add value or cut expenses or both.

Whilst this book is primarily about marketing, there are lots of other ways to increase the value of a business. Operationally or financially, the scope of improvements are outside this text but when you look at a business to acquire, you should at least have some kind of basic checklist to see where you (or your existing organisation or portfolio) can add value ...

Ways to Add Value to a Business

- Improve marketing. Increase customers and referrals and upsell/cross-sell/down-sell/identify USPs/closer alignment with clients' needs/reward loyalty.

- Improve service(s). Innovation/quality/convenience/ simplicity/speed/customer-experience/fun/friendliness (i.e. humanise)/variety/expertise/packaging/design/ communications/functionality/after-sales.

- Better staffing. Train better or hire better. Continual development. Be a better leader.

- Improve operation. Identify ways to increase value along the value chain.

- Better financing. Raise prices, make payments easy and offer choices and terms.

- Strategic ventures. Improve synergies with other businesses (especially ones you own) in terms of

customers/suppliers/staff/sales/marketing/operations/
logistics/administration.

Ways to Cut Costs from a Business

- De-duplication. E.g. by sharing a single book-keeper or premises with the existing company. Consider all the cost-centres that can be de-duplicated. Sharing software or other resources with another business - where legal - can be advantageous.

- Remove/replace unnecessary/underperforming management, consultants and staff.

- Consider paying management/staff/consultants/suppliers based on performance.

- Sack bad clients. Poor payers/time-consumers/'whingers' (make a judgement call!)

- Ditto bad suppliers. Remove ones which are unreliable/inflexible/overly-expensive or provide too little value for their cost.

- Consider outsourcing some operations to interns or freelancers or overseas workers.

- Pay for the 'job done' rather than the 'time taken'.

- Staff monitoring. Track attendance at work, output, personal calls, social media, emails, sick days, 'meetings', timekeeping, lunch-breaks etc.

- Reduce overtime or extra/unnecessary hours.

- "Freebies". Be vigilant for theft, fraud, inflated expenses, plagiarism, nepotism etc.

- Virtualisation. Work from home/cheaper premises, for yourself and key people.

- Leverage dead space. Charge for storage/desking etc.

- Consider using second-hand equipment. Check out auctions. Try borrowing stuff.

- Buy in bulk. Consider joint-venturing with others for discounts (even competitors).

- Optimise marketing costs and continually improve them.

- Sponsorships. Get your suppliers to contribute towards marketing costs.

- Grants. Check to see whether there are grants (or other funding) available.

- Tax. Be as ruthless as possible whilst remaining legal. Get the best advice.

- Reduce debts where possible/financially sensible to do so.

- Continually prune or renegotiate contracts or terms for utilities/rents/supplies/stock/services etc. Set aside a regular time-slot to review your expenses.

- Streamline operations. Use technology. Automate, systemise.

- Leverage online. Sales/marketing/payments/ purchasing/meetings/communications (internal and external)/processes (e.g. book keeping).

- Bartering. Pay supplies with stuff you can get cheap, effectively giving you a discount.

- Payments in. Strive to have your invoice paid faster or better still, immediately.

- Payments out. Consider paying bills later or negotiate discount for early payments. Reward staff when they identify ways to save costs while maintaining quality.

5
Finding
(Sourcing Deals)

The key to getting a good deal is being exposed to *lots of deals*, from the right places.

By ensuring you have a deal-pipeline in place, you're not just dependent on those occasional deals that land at your feet, for which you'd likely be too grateful for and too attached to. Often, the best business is *no business at all* and being able to walk away is very powerful in terms of your positioning and negotiation.

To generate deal-flow, there must be activity on your part, at least until people start bringing opportunities to you. Here are a few ways to source businesses to acquire, although there are as many ways to source them as there are businesses themselves, so don't be too rigid in your thinking.

Remember, any business person you meet could potentially sell you their business, if the conditions were favourable and they were *asked in the first place*.

Business Brokers

Generally speaking, by the time a business is listed with a business broker, the asking price will be at a premium and getting a 'bargain' will be much harder, due to competition. The broker has already 'sold the dream' to the vendor and they will have been primed to expect a life-changing cash sum. As always, there are exceptions to the rule and you can work with brokers to your advantage. Notwithstanding this, if there is a business that is highly important to you because of its strategic value, then you may simply want to pay full market value and get one 'off the shelf' without the hassle of sourcing one for yourself. Brokers have a constant stream of businesses to sell and they can keep you in the loop. Brokers have the advantage that they are already working with multiple vendors, they can give you lofts of information ready to go plus they are financially motivated themselves to sell the business. However, never forget that they are always acting in the interests of themselves and/or the vendor. They can often give a false impression of the value of the business and also the amount of interest it is receiving.

If possible, ensure that any brokers you are working with are accredited with bodies such as the International Business Brokers Association (IBBA) or NAEA Commercial. Members of such bodies are subject to a code of conduct and membership indicates that they have the necessary professional skills, knowledge and experience.

There are various websites that list businesses for sale. As a bare minimum, check out:

Businessesforsale.com

bizbuysell.com

daltonsbusiness.com

rightbiz.co.uk

gumtree.com/business-for-sale

When you register for these sites, you get alerts when prospects that match your criteria are added and at the very least, you can start to get an industry-feel for what sums businesses are asking for and you can scrutinise their numbers in terms of profits, turnover etc.

Interestingly, the majority of businesses sold are not via brokers at all, they are sold privately.

Private Sales - Acquiring Businesses that are not Listed for Sale Anywhere

Ideally, you'll be working with a *motivated seller* because you want to acquire your target business for as little as possible. If you can acquire a business at a discount, you're already ahead of the game and less financially exposed. If the motivated seller hasn't listed their business with any of the brokers or broker websites, there should be less competition (ideally none) and hopefully you'll get a better deal.

Below are a few of the main reasons a business owner may be motivated to sell, other than simply cashing-out a profitable business (or selling because the offer is too good to refuse).

- Retirement.

- Cash problems. Tax issues. Out of control personal finances. Litigation.

- Health issues.

- Poor performance/declining revenues.

- Boredom/tired owner/'burnout'.

- Life changing event: relocation, family illness, divorce, etc.

- New horizons.

- Partner disputes.

- Industry changes, new legislation or industry downturn.

From this short list, we can see some motivational causes have less impact on the value of a business than others. Someone telling us that they're looking for a new challenge may sound plausible but we need to ensure they're not trying to cover-up a more sinister reason that they're keen to sell. Much like buying a second-hand car, it's a case of 'caveat emptor'. More about this later in the section about due diligence.

So, where do you find these business owners that are motivated to sell their business? The simple answer is *anywhere and everywhere.*

Whilst we'll shortly examine some simple strategies to methodically search for these motivated sellers, the fact is that you should always be open-minded and available to a potential deal in any situation where you're interacting with other people, even if they're not the business owner themselves. Of course, you'll most likely be in a traditional business environment such as meeting with clients but don't forget that all business owners have private lives too and so you could easily hear or see signs of an opportunity whilst you're playing golf or at a wedding or pretty much anywhere else.

Always be alert to signals heralding an opportunity. You may not directly hear someone exclaim out loud that they're desperate to sell their business but you may well overhear them saying that they need to start caring for a family member or move location or that they have health issues. Put two and two together and voila ... you may just have a lead. Clearly, discretion is called for!

Given what you now know about direct response marketing, you should now be in a position to devise a basic strategy for both inbound and/or outbound marketing ... ideally both. For starters, we can consider channels such as:

Channels

- Offline ads. Trade publications, journals, portal sites etc.

- Online ads. Search ads (Google/Bing PPC), Facebook ads, site-sponsored ads, YouTube ads etc.

- Social media. Both ads and engagement on Facebook, LinkedIn, Reddit etc.

- Social groups. Facebook groups, LinkedIn groups, meetups, specialist blogs/sites etc.

- Word of mouth. Customers, suppliers, business owners,

competitors, brokers etc.

- Trade shows, sponsored events, business networking.
- Business buyers' clubs/associations.
- Mailing lists.

There will be many more, although you now have plenty to be getting on with.

Targets for Directing Your Communications

Competitors, accountants, commercial solicitors, business brokers, administrators, financial advisors, other 'deal makers' (sourcers), business consultants and coaches ...

We're talking about essentially putting up a sign that says, 'sell us your business' and while your ideal vendors could be anywhere, you should ideally advertise where your *target market* will be lurking so you get the most 'bang for your buck'. This can mean industry magazines or websites/portals or indeed any of the channels mentioned earlier.

As well as advertising the fact you're an investor looking to acquire a business, you should also *read* those same publications/websites as they may well have listings for sale.

Walking around trade shows can be a rich source of pickings as you'll often be talking directly with the people you need to deal with. Remember, whether you meet people at a trade show or conference or wherever, you're *playing the long game*. It's likely the people you talk with may not have thought about selling (or at least not there and then) and so it's important to *retain their contact information* so that you can maintain communications over time.

Also, always remember to ask the question "Do you know anyone *else* that might be interested in selling?", because you'll address a wider audience and - in conjunction with your follow-up communications, you'll be giving people the chance to let the idea *sink in* (for selling their own business) and harness their network of other potential business vendors. Plus, if there's a commission in it for them, they may be more predisposed to develop keener ears to listen out for opportunities for you.

Your word of mouth marketing and social media activity will be enhanced when you make it apparent in the first place and then *reiterate* that you're an investor looking for an opportunities in 'X' industry and that you'll reward people for passing opportunities your way.

Let's take a moment to look at some simple outbound communications by means of identifying a list of suitable people to approach and then contacting them, which can be a very successful strategy, endorsed by a number of successful, serial entrepreneurs.

You can start by simply writing a letter (yes, an old fashioned, printed letter) to a target list and ask them if they'd consider selling their business. Tell them you're looking to invest in their business and that you'd like to discuss it with them. When contacting people for the first time, it's essential to remember to 'sell' the idea of having an initial phone-call. Keep the outbound message short, simple, to the point, respectful (remembering to ask if they know anyone else that may be interested in selling their business) and ever so slightly *humble*. Highlight the fact you're an individual (rather than a corporate purchaser) and that you're in a position to move quickly and would love to have a quick chat to explore options.

Much like the direct marketing covered elsewhere in this book, your results will be improved when you follow up with a phone-call and/or another direct mail piece. It not only shows that you're serious but, once again, it will give the idea time to *sink in*.

Whilst you can get a list of business from (reputable) list-brokers, I have found that very often they don't list many of the businesses that I'd have expected to find there. For that reason, you may wish to augment their data with lists you've compiled from trade directories, chambers of commerce, web listings, LinkedIn … and good old Google. It's important you're writing to the correct person (i.e. the owner) and that you write *personally* rather than in an overly corporate style.

Franky, I'd spend the most time on this strategy because it directly communicates to the people that you'd want to speak with (technically they're your competitors, assuming you're acquiring in the same vertical). You could take the view that passing any business to a competitor is strengthening them against you. I take a different stance.

Even if passing a lead across doesn't result in an outright business sale, I believe it's good to establish and maintain a healthy, patent dialogue with your competitors because it is entirely possible to conduct profitable business with them. Rather than blindly 'slugging it out' for the same clients, it can be a lot more beneficial to try and *work with* your competition. You can pass sales leads between each other on the occasions that the business is not quite right for one party but ideal for the other.

For example, sometimes, no matter how hard you try, a potential client simply won't buy from you. Pass it along and at least one of you gets something from the sale. Furthermore, there may well be products and/or services that you offer or need that the 'competitor' wants or needs that you can do a deal on. Plus, if either of you changes your mind about selling (or buying) the other's business at any stage in the future, you'll be a lot more kindly disposed towards the other party if you've maintained good relations.

Other Potential Sources

Business doesn't operate in a vacuum and there are plenty of other people that are directly connected with companies that you may be interested in acquiring. So, ask for their help.

Having already mentioned to your own sphere of influence that you're looking to invest (clients, suppliers, competitors and the like) you can now start to enlist an army of *other strategic partners* such as solicitors, accountants, business advisors, consultants, IFA's, insolvency practitioners, retirement specialists ... i.e., anyone who is likely in contact with your potential vendors.

By joining some of the various business buyers' clubs/groups available, you'll also meet other 'dealmakers' and it can be a good strategy to swap leads, pool resources and even share stories with them, as they may have exactly the deal you're looking for. At the very least, you can learn from each other. To this end, there are various Facebook groups, LinkedIn groups and websites you can join (often for free) and a quick search will prove invaluable.

6
Qualification

Assuming you're actively, consistently prospecting, sooner or later you'll start getting leads.

You'll need to process and filter them as efficiently as possible otherwise your time can evaporate, leaving you little time for anything else. Having established your 'filters' (according to your own business criteria established earlier) you're now in a position to start having those initial phone-calls. Early on, you'll need to establish the seller's price expectations. They will very likely be a first-time seller and whilst some people understand what realistic market prices are for their industry, many won't.

Things to Listen Out For - Over the Phone

At this stage, you're looking to just get a very rough idea of who they are and what they want. You'll be discussing sensitive information with people that you've never met before so be as polite, respectful and reassuring as possible. You don't want them to have any reasons to feel any more awkward than they already do. Even if you decide that you're not interested, it never does any harm to remain friendly, courteous, respectful and approachable, after all they may come back with a revised schedule or know someone else looking to sell.

Even at this early stage, you may be required to sign a non-disclosure agreement (NDA), so be prepared for that and check that it contains no onerous terms before signing. Better still, make it *your* NDA and offer it up front.

Whilst trying to establish their *goals*, their *reasons* for selling, their *urgency* and their *values*, the words they use will be revealing. Use open-ended questions as much as possible and try and build trust quickly. Rapport is essential and will be instrumental if you proceed to the negotiation stage. It helps if you're not a closed book and so you should tell them a bit about yourself and let them understand that you're a human being, not some corporate monster looking to devour small business owners. Refer to the rapport building section earlier on in section one of this book.

At the initial phone call stage, you're looking for the following information:

- **Who** they are (and who else is involved in their business).
- **What** their business is: preliminary details (see below).
- **Why** they're interested in potentially selling their business.
- **When** they're looking to exit.
- **How** much … a rough idea of their expectations (don't get too drawn into this yet).

Note, due to time constraints, you won't be able meet every business owner that expresses an interest in selling which is why a phone-filtering session is important. However, until you're more polished in this process, it might be a useful exercise to meet a few for discussions face to face, even if it leads to nothing, just for *the practice.*

Obviously, what you're looking for is a business owner that would be willing to sell you their business at the right price, in the right way. If you can establish a deal where you pay very little upfront and make *deferred payments* from future profits, then you may well have hit the jackpot. However the business is paid for, its saleprice is simply what it's worth to you and what it's worth to others, hackneyed as that is.

Snap-Valuing a Business

In order to make any decisions, you'll need some numbers (see below). If the person on the phone doesn't have that information to hand it's not necessarily a problem, but they'll certainly need to get you those figures before you continue.

You need to ask about the financial state of the business. Management accounts are 'malleable' and cash-flow is very different to profit ... so ask to see the bank statements! Remember, you're looking for a business that can either be fixed (and thus bought cheaply) or which is financially healthy (and you're buying it for the instant profits). Look for healthy margins (so you can make healthy profits if/when the business is 'fixed'), assets (so you can raise capital if necessary) and recurring revenues models, (so you can have or develop steady cash-flow).

Run a stress testing/sensitivity analysis. What would the figures look like if 20% were added to costs or if the sales dropped by 20% ... or both?

Note - financial issues can be in a poor state, that doesn't mean it's not fixable and may well provide reason(s) to acquire the business cheaply. However, you need to *ensure that it is fixable*. For example, a business may have good cash-flow and contracts in place but have poor margins which could be fixed by increasing prices and service and/or reducing overheads. However, if market forces determine that the margins cannot be improved, then you can't fix it ... so walk away. By way of another example, if the business has no assets (e.g. no contracts in place) then you'll have a much harder job to raise funds against the business so you'd have to use your own money to invest (not a smart move) and clients could walk away post-purchase ... again, avoid.

There are a few ways to value a business. It's important to look at the potential value of a business through different lenses, if nothing else because it'll give you a more balanced view. Certainly, the banks (and other lenders) won't have as optimistic view as the vendor, broker or possibly even you and they'll potentially charge from £2K to £20K just to value the business so it makes sense to quickly get a handle on the *book value* (i.e. the net asset value) which is the method they use. Accountants typically use the NBV method as well.

Note, if/when you pay for an appraisal, you retain control and can keep it to yourself. You can share it with the vendor if it helps your cause (bearing in mind there's a risk they could use that information for other buyers). If the vendor pays for the appraisal, it will likely be biased.

The book value valuation method coldly looks at the value of the company's cash and other *realisable* assets (e.g. stock, equipment, receivables etc), minus all liabilities (debts, depreciation, wages, taxes etc). This method will typically provide the lowest value of a business which is why banks and other lenders use it, after all they'll want their money back if there has to be a 'fire-sale'.

It's important to look at assets objectively. Just because a business owner spent (say) £50k on a stunning trade exhibition display, it doesn't mean it's worth anything to the bank or indeed anyone else.

On the other end of the spectrum, most business owners like to think that the value of their business should be reflected in terms of historic goodwill, future cash-flows and potential. The trouble is, you can't cash goodwill at the bank.

Multiples of net profits (more specifically, it's usually quoted as EBITDA - Earnings Before Interest, Tax, Depreciation and Amortisation) is probably the valuation method that's most banded around. You can Google the specific multiplier for your industry. Remember that for smaller businesses, you'll need to adjust for the owner's salary/drawings and insert the relevant salary for an 'off-the-shelf managing director' to arrive at a more accurate profit figure, adding any significant assets such as property.

Finally, consider the *entry cost valuation*. i.e., how much money (and time) would it cost you to create and build up a similar business from scratch?

In reality, the minimum and maximum values you'll arrive at will be derived from referencing a mixture of the above models. There are others models too. You'll likely look at how much the business has been making over recent years (and how much the owner has been taking out), look at the industry EBITDA multiplier, add book value (or subtract debts) and compare with other businesses in the sector while taking a view of other factors such as:

- Age of the business and its reputation/goodwill.

- Opportunity to improve future cash-flows and profits.

- Industry trends and comparables.

- Reason(s) the business is being sold.

- Relationships with clients, suppliers, staff.

- Strategic value to you.

Tip - Remember goodwill as the ability to earn a premium. In a service based industry, evaluation of intangible assets is far more important. This could be location, branding, customer perception etc. The value of the employees is often overlooked. Their skill/morale needs to be assessed.

If projections don't show enough profit levels, examine what would be needed to achieve the profit, don't simply increase projected revenues. Obviously, if it doesn't work ... walk.

Businesses to Avoid

- Too expensive. Likely over- valued by a sentimental owner. Or via another 'dealer' or broker.

- Overly in debt, or about to be in debt soon (e.g. an imminent tax liability).

- Too few assets. No property or contracts or stock or debtors to leverage against.

- Poor reputation. A bad reputation can be hard to shake off, if ever.

- Poor staff. If it's not just one or two, rehiring can be overly expensive and/or time consuming.

- Revenues which are low or unstable or with low margins that can't be fixed.

- Complex ownership structures e.g. other family members, investors, distant shareholders etc.

- Insurmountable, upcoming legal issues challenges from customers, staff, suppliers, general public etc.

- Unreasonable owners. Won't give you information or stick to agreements or who are disruptive etc.

- No contracts or security in place for staff or clients etc. People can simply walk after the sale.

Trust your gut instincts ... ask yourself: "Does the business stack up? Do I get a bad feeling about it? Can I work with the vendor and do I get a good feeling about them?"

Consider hiring a business broker to consult with you, especially if it's your first purchase. You could accelerate your learning and get a professional to help you, one that is *not financially motivated by the sale* and only gets paid for the independent advice they dispense.

7
Negotiation and Offer

If your 'napkin valuation' stacks up, then the next step is to meet the seller for a face to face meeting and take it to the next stage, namely to gain more information (you've only got very rudimentary information so far, likely from over the phone and Google) and proceed to *negotiate*, potentially *making an offer* (next).

As mentioned already, the key to negotiation is *rapport*. It's critical to 'sell yourself to the seller', otherwise all bets are off. Re-read the section in this book about developing rapport (if you haven't done so already). Both of you will be nervous. You'll have to ask lots of questions. Rapport will help when you uncover certain truths and awkward silences (potentially indicating a way to get a better price).

Arrange to initially meet the vendor for tea/coffee, somewhere neutral. Ideally somewhere close to their business, so you can go there later if things go well. Be mindful that the vendor probably won't want any staff knowing the reason for your visit, just yet anyway. If you can, sit at a corner of a table with them or on the same side (as if you're both looking at, say, a laptop). This is more conducive to a spirit of collaboration than when you both have a large table between you (especially at either party's premises) which can feel a lot more confrontational, according to behaviourists. Certainly 'getting people on side' helps in a literal sense when it comes to sales in other settings.

When you arrive, don't just dive straight in, take time to 'warm up' and use that opportunity to find out about the seller and try and establish some commonalities. Topics to include during early conversations can be about people, places, values, likes, dislikes, challenges etc.

Some Rapport Building Questions

- What are their interests?

- How did they get involved with the business?

- Why did you decide to work in [vendor's field]?

- Are their friends or family involved?

- What were their original goals for the business?

- How have things changed?

- What achievements whilst running it are they most proud of?

- What would they do differently?

Tip - use positive language - not negative - and avoid 'seller's remorse'.

Later on in your conversation, you can ask more aspirational, future-pacing questions questions like:

- What would they like to do next?

- What's holding them back from reaching their goals?

- If they don't solve [problem], what kind of difficulties will they have moving forward?

- What won't happen that they want to happen?

Ask *"Tell me more?"* or *"How so?"* or *"Please elaborate,"* for any answers that would benefit from more explanation.

If the business is distressed, the owner will likely feel as though they have a millstone around their neck. They're in 'survival mode' and consequently not necessarily thinking about alternative solutions. Try and take them from 'survival' thinking to 'possibility' thinking.

Remember to focus your attention (and dialogue) on the seller's problems and not your own. Later on, show the other person how *their* needs will be met.

For instance, you can ask them, *"If we could work with each other to help you exit your current difficulties, what would it mean for you, personally?"*

Once you've invested time to understand them and hopefully established some common ground, you'll need to ask the more probing questions about their business and what they want from it. Understand that in order to progress, you'll need to *give information* as well as take it. The vendor will have questions and concerns. It will help if you're prepared for them and can see things from their point of view.

What the Seller Might Be Thinking (Or Worried About)

Questions most likely to be asked of you:

- "Why do you want to buy my business?"
- "How much is my business worth?"
- "What will you do with my business?"
- "What about my team?"
- "How can I be sure of what you say?"

This is only the tip of the iceberg. Here are a few more worries that the seller may be thinking about (but not necessarily saying them out loud).

- Am I doing the right thing?
- Will I regret this?
- [Ego] Do I want this person to make my business more successful than me?
- How long will all of this take?

- Am I selling at the right time?

- Am I selling too cheaply?

- What are my tax liabilities?

- Will I be liable for any future problems in the business?

- Do I trust this person? Am I selling to the wrong person?

- Will I ever get paid? Will I get paid all my future instalments?

- Are they going to just asset-strip the business and leave me holding the liabilities?

- What if they breach confidentiality?

- What will become of me ... and my life ... after I leave the business?

- Will I lose my identity or self-worth when I'm no longer the boss?

- I've so much to do, will this sales process will distract me from my work?

- Will I look stupid? Do I know what I'm doing ... this is all very confusing?

- My company and my finances are in a mess ... what will people think?

- What will happen to the people I care about?

- Will I be expected to 'work for' the new boss?

- What if they discover *that issue we don't talk about* ... what do I say?

- How will they do it? What're they hiding? What are their plans?

Be careful; if you explain in any great detail about how you intend to improve the business, the vendor might decide to either do it themselves or even potentially use that information to attract/help other potential buyers (who will likely be your competition) which can ultimately hurt you.

Try and reassure the vendor about their team/staff (especially if you're hoping the vendor to finance the deal) but don't commit yourself or back yourself in a corner should you need to make changes to the team, which you very possibly will.

Without being robotic, you should find out the answers to the relevant questions (below). Depending on how your initial meeting goes, it's likely that some of these questions will be asked later on, in other meeting.

Generic Questions to Find Out About a Business

⇨ The Seller

- What is the seller's area of expertise?
- Will they be available to consult with after the sale?
- Who else is involved in the business or who has a financial or legal interest in the sale?
- Any there any share ownership disputes: historic, ongoing or oncoming?

⇨ The Sale of The Company

- How much are they asking for the sale?
- What's are their expected payment terms?
- How flexible / negotiable are they?
- Why are they looking to sell at this time?
- What's not included in the sale of the business?

- Are they looking to sell the assets or shares or what? Why is that important to you?

- How did they calculate the asking price? Was it an external appraisal - can they share it?

- What's the history of the business? How long has the current owner run the company?

- Who else is/was involved with the business?

- What's the legal structure of the business?

- Any ownership/shares disputes: historic, ongoing or oncoming?

⇨ **The Marketing**

- Who is involved in this part of the business?

- Who/which/where are their target market(s)?

- Who are their typical clients?

- How big is their target market?

- What is their market share?

- In what geographical area(s) do they engage in business?

- What are other potential target markets/ areas/niches/ sectors?

- What do their target market(s) want?

- How do they know what they want?

- What are their main USPs?

- How do their clients perceive them? Positioning? High-end, mid-range, cheap?

- What products or services do they sell?

- What's the most profitable product/service they provide

and the ratio of these to total sales?

- What's their main offer to attract new business?

- How satisfied are the customers?

- What referral and testimonial systems are in place?

- How well are testimonials and referrals coming in?

- Who are the key influencers in their industry?

- Which strategic alliances or joint ventures are in place and with whom?

- What do customers like most about their products or services or industry at large?

- What do customers dislike most about their products or services or industry at large?

- What is better or unique about their services and/or products?

- Why do customers buy its products or use its services?

- What's the average lifetime of their client relationship? Average lifetime value?

- How well and often do they currently communicate with them? Via which media?

- What systems or software do they use to manage their client database?

- How do they market to (and manage opportunities for) existing clients?

- How do they market to potential clients?

- What marketing channels have they used that worked? Costs? Conversion rates?

- What marketing have they used that didn't work? Costs?

Conversion rates?

- What is the URL/address of their main website(s)?

- Do they have access to statistics for their website?

- Why hasn't the business grown bigger? (Careful not to antagonise the vendor.)

- What marketing software/systems/processes are in place? How effective are they?

- Which marketing software/systems/processes are documented and available?

- Are there any particular problems/limitations or concerns to be aware of?

⇨ The Sales

- Who is involved in sales?

- What are the sales figures for existing clients?

- What are the sales figures for new clients?

- How long is the average sales lifecycle?

- Where/how do they get their opportunities (existing business) and leads (new business)?
  What are their sales activities?

- What are their conversion rates?

- What are their targets/commissions/bonuses etc?

- Any particular problems/limitations or concerns to be aware of?

⇨ The Operations and Deliverables

- Who is involved in this part of the business?

- What products and services are offered?

- How are they delivered?

- What are the quality control process?

- What operational software/systems/processes are in place? How effective are they?

- Which operational software/systems/processes are documented and available?

- Any particular problems/limitations or concerns to be aware of?

⇨ The Administration

- Who is involved in this part of the business?

- What administration software/systems/processes are in place? How effective are they?

- Are they documented and available?

- Any particular administration problems/limitations or concerns to be aware of?

⇨ The Finances

- Who is involved in this part of the business?

- What are the revenues and gross/net profits for recent years?

- What are the regular fixed running costs? Rent, rates, utilities, wages, debt-payments etc.

- What are the regular variable costs? Materials, commissions, licences, costs/unit/etc.

- What are irregular costs? Irregular liabilities, refunds, capital expenditure etc.

- What products/services are sold and their respective costs/margins?

- Ask for full access to the key financial information (refer the due diligence section).

- What financial software/systems/processes are in place? How effective are they?

- Are they documented and available?

- Any particular financial problems/limitations or concerns to be aware of?

⇨ The Training

- Who is involved in this part of the business?

- What training programme is currently in place? What training is mandatory? What training is voluntary?

- What skills/qualifications/experience do staff require to start working there?

- What skills/qualifications/experience do staff acquire whilst working there?

- Which training procedures are documented and available?

- What's the key industry media? Online portals, events, shows, printed material etc.

- What training software/systems/processes are in place? How effective are they?

- Are they documented and available?

- Any particular problems/limitations or concerns to be aware of?

⇨ The Competition

- What's the health of the industry?

- What are the industry average costs, pay, turnover etc?

- Who are their main competitors? Why are they successful?

- How many new companies are opening?

- Which products/services/geographic-areas/industry sub-sectors have the *most* competition?

- The least?

- Do they currently work with any competitors? If so, how?

- Which competitors have they had difficulties with? Any disputes: historic, ongoing or oncoming?

⇨ The Staff

- Who's involved in the business and what do they do?

- What's the team structure?

- What is done in house and what is outsourced?

- What sub-contractors, consultants are used?

- What do the owner(s) pay themselves in wages, profits, 'perks' and other benefits?

- How are staff paid and what are their terms?

- What's the situation for payroll, benefits, perks, vacations, pensions etc?

- Which staff are indispensable and why?

- How insulated is the business against sudden migration of key suppliers?

- Which staff have they had difficulties with? Any disputes: historic, ongoing or oncoming?

⇨ The Customers

- Who are their best customers?

- How much do their *best* customers spend? (Watch out for over-reliance on key customers)

- Do any key clients represent a large chunk of the total revenue? i.e., more than, say, 15%?

- Who are their *average* customers?

- What do their customers expect from them? What do they expect from their customers?

- What are their payment terms?
  Other terms? (deliverables/timescales/refund-policy etc).

- Which customers have they had difficulties with?
  Any disputes: historic, ongoing or oncoming?

⇨ The Suppliers

- Which suppliers are involved and what are their terms? How negotiable are they?

- What issues will you need to know for contracts/ insurances/securities/disclaimers etc?

- How insulated is the business against a sudden migration of key suppliers?

- Which suppliers are good/reliable? Poor/unreliable?

- Which suppliers have they had difficulties with?
  Any disputes: historic, ongoing or oncoming?

⇨ Other Stakeholders

- Who else is impacted by the business? e.g., neighbours, other businesses, community etc.

- How good is their relationship with the tax-man?

- Is the business involved in any corporate social responsibility initiatives?

- Does the business give (or receive) any awards, grants, industry recognition etc?

- Is the business part of any other organisations, memberships, initiatives etc?

⇨ Other Questions

- What areas within the company do they consider need improving and why?

- What are their plans after selling the business?

- What would they change about the business and the industry?

- How is the industry performing at large?

- Identify any internal and external SWOTs: strengths, weaknesses, opportunities, threats.

- Identify any PEST issues: political, environmental, social, technological.

- What are their expectations and requirements within the whole business-sale process?

- What type of person do they believe would be the best to inherit the business?

- What would they like to achieve over the next 90 days?

- If they've had previous negotiations, how did they go?

- If the negotiation is successful, how do they see the transition happening?

- Will they provide access to financial, management and other accounts during due-diligence?

And ... leave this killer question until last ... Is there anything - as yet undiscussed - that will come to light during the due-diligence process? *Watch their reaction carefully.*

When Speaking with the Seller

Negotiation isn't conflict. Try and avoid thinking in terms of win-lose and instead think in terms of win-win. Use collaborative and positive words like agreement, brainstorming, collaborate, synergy, alliance, teamwork, cooperation, mutual, us, we, our, join, play, ideas, fun. Conversely, avoid antagonistic words like accept/reject, win/lose, buyout, takeover etc.

Listen to the seller's *needs*. Ask open ended questions. Watch their body language. When you ask a question met with emotion, silence or awkwardness, back off for a bit. If necessary, go back later after a day or so. But don't give up, keep trying. Make sure you understand the root of any issues (assuming they're not simply frustrated/insulted by the questions).

It's important to keep in mind that somewhere, their business will have flaws. Weaknesses in the seller are reflected in their business. Don't criticise! It is their 'baby', they will almost certainly have strong emotional ties and any perceived attacks/criticisms will likely be counter-productive (even if you're simply trying to get a better price).

Choose your words carefully and frame things so as not to appear to be a criticism of their character. Address and highlight any problems you uncover in the first person and don't apportion blame or criticise the owner.

For instance: "The management accounts are terrible," could well be considered antagonising, where "If full management accounts were available, it'd help us both," may prove less jarring.

Once you have uncovered as much information as you can about the business in order to make a valuation for yourself, you'll be in a position to negotiate the price and the terms and - if all goes well - make an offer. Obviously, any offer you make will be subject to your due diligence process (below).

Tip - *Remove emotions* from all your considerations. It's easy to get too attached to a deal. Have a financial framework in place that you stick to and if the numbers don't stack, walk away.

A full treatise on negotiation is outside the scope of this text, so I've included a number of *essentials* to consider. The starting point is to *do your homework.*

Know Yourself. Know Them. Know the Business. Know the Market.

That's been borrowed a little from 'The Art of War' by Sun Tzu. Whilst I'm not advocating being combative at all (quite the opposite), certainly knowing the 'terrain' of the business environment and the strengths and weaknesses within yourself and that of the other person will prove invaluable.

Find out what they want! Ask open-ended questions. There's what they'll tell you, then there's what they want. Then there's what they *really, really* want, as per the song. Understand as much as you can before your meeting and do your research: social media websites, their own website, background reading, asking other people.

Clearly, we're trying to establish as much as we can about the business, the vendor, the environment etc. yet it can be easy to overlook the fact that we should *know ourselves*. That is to say, we need to know our strengths, weaknesses, what we're prepared to do and - more importantly - we need to know (and stick to) what we're *not prepared to do*.

Knowing our starting and finishing points are vital. How many people visit an auction and end up paying way more than they had intended to? Consider your BATNA's (Best Alternative to A Negotiated Agreement). What are your (best) alternatives to what's being offered? Again, simply knowing that you do have alternatives (e.g. knowing other companies that are for sale and their asking-prices or knowing the costs of building up a client base without an acquisition) gives you power.

Come from a position of *strength*. Have alternatives in place i.e. a 'pipeline' of other deals. Understand there will always be another deal. Communicate your strength (subtly, without any bravado) and avoid weak language (e.g. "I hate to ask but ... ").

Don't be afraid to ask for what you want. Don't undervalue yourself. Aim high and expect the best outcome. Be able to say 'no' to terms you don't like. Ultimately, *be able to walk away*.

Remember your key bargaining chips: You're not a corporate investor so you offer ease of negotiation, flexibility, speed and (if you're buying directly) you'll save them broker fees.

Inoculate the vendor. In the first instance, the vendor has the power to simply not sell their business to you so you must demonstrate utmost respect and make them like you. However, at some point(s) during the buying process (which can take a long time) it's very likely that patience will get frayed, emotions will run high and things can be said in the heat of the moment. This is common but you don't want to get derailed so you need to take the lead and explain up front that there will be challenges and perhaps even arguments. It's part and parcel of it all so make sure they're prepared for the rollercoaster of dealing with you.

Given that this whole process can be stressful, beware of emotions from the seller as well as yourself. Thus, 'inoculating' the vendor up-front means explaining that you'll be honest and fair and that you'll do everything you can to make things as smooth as possible but that sometimes things can get heated. Explain to them that it's normal and that nothing is ever to be taken personally. This helps them to be less likely to over react if/when it happens. Remind them that people are emotional and buying/selling a business is an emotive experience and that - when they're past all the awkwardness, you can crack open a bottle of bubbly and (hopefully) celebrate together.

Control the time and place. Suggest a place - ideally neutral (initially at least). Offer a few alternative time slots. Conversely, if these are offered to you, be busy! i.e. don't appear to have an empty diary.

Don't appear in a hurry (unless that is to your advantage). Ideally, choose *nice weather* (it's more conducive to collaboration). If you *must* negotiate in bad weather, take a moment to discuss the bad weather before the negotiation, as it will help neutralise any associated bad moods/feelings. This is more important than it sounds.

Get the 'yesses' out of the way. It's been demonstrated that when people agree with (several) small things and say 'yes', they're more likely to say yes later on to bigger requests. Innocuous looking questions such as "Shall we sit here?" or "The weather is terrible, isn't it?" can actually be used as part of a 'yes set'. It's a good idea to first cover the small negotiable issues where you can quickly make ground and gain small agreements.

Counter offers. If you simply accept what is being offered without making counter-offers, you will have lost the potential for a better deal and additionally, the vendor will assume they could have made a better deal for themselves, which can create remorse. Even if their offer is fantastic, at the very least, pause for a few seconds before accepting. This will let them know that you've mulled-over their offer (without instantly accepting) and during the natural tension, they may even blurt something out that works in your favour.

Meet concessions with requests. Negotiation is a tit-for-tat process. If they ask you to do something, ask for something in return. For example, if they ask you to increase your cash-offer, suggest that you'll increase your overall payment if the company performs better than promised. If you have to make concessions, make them in installments as it has more impact. It's been shown that people are happier to find two £10 notes consecutively than one £20 note.

Don't have a 'one-thing' mindset. Focusing just on monetary values can stifle creativity and limit good negotiation. Negotiate on *other terms*. List out things that are important to you and rank them in order of importance. Ask them to do the same. See where you can be flexible and trade concessions important to them yet only incidental to you. And vice-versa.

Bundling and unbundling terms. People can be influenced by the number of items in a list. For example, a simple (but often inaccurate) heuristic people use when looking at similar products in a catalogue, is the length of the list of features. Those items with a longer list can appear to have more value. When trading concessions as part of your negotiations, you can make one concession that you offer appear more appealing by repackaging it as more concessions in a list.

For example, if one of the elements you were offering as part of a deal to purchase a company was to retain the staff, this could be unbundled as honour the employment contracts with existing staff, honour their holiday liabilities, honour their sickness benefits, honour their pension provisions ... etc. It's the same thing, simply drawn out, for more perceived value.

Conversely, if someone has provided a list of concessions that fall into a common topic, these can be bundled together, thus shortening the list and reducing their impact.

Employ primacy and recency. Whilst you're ideally not 'pitching' to buy their business against other competitors, it's helpful to remember that when people are considering multiple proposals for the same thing, they will quickly forget a lot of the information.

Often, they'll give disproportionate attention to the first thing/ proposal/person (primacy) and the last one (recency). As an aside, it's probably why giving someone bad news is sometimes best delivered as part of a so-called 'sh*t sandwich', which takes the format: good news, bad news, good news.

E.g., "Hello Mr Johnson. The boss was impressed by your performance this quarter although he couldn't accede to your request for a pay-rise just yet. However, he said you can definitely expect a raise soon."

Reciprocity. Listed among other principles in Dr. Cialdini's excellent book about persuasion (reciprocity, commitment/

consistency, social proof, authority, liking, scarcity), we find that reciprocity can have a powerful effect within negotiations, particularly when used as part of a set. Giving people insights into your personal life (e.g. a few issues you've had to deal with or mistakes you've made) can help show you're human, and engender reciprocity.

Also, food helps! Consider taking your vendor out for a hot meal or at the very least a hot drink (tea, coffee). Look at the benefits: a lack of distractions (hopefully), convivial (i.e., non-competitive) surroundings, feelings of warmth (experiencing physical warmth can help associate warm feelings towards you), a sense of reciprocity and lastly it will *raise their blood sugar levels*. Think about what you are like when your blood sugar levels are low compared to when you've just eaten.

Justify with data, charts and graphs. People can often more readily accept (and be led by) arguments that include 'scientific looking' evidence such as data, statistics, charts, graphs and quotes from respected people.

Verbal cues, body language ... and all that jazz. As so much information is available about the non-verbal cues we should be able to detect when negotiating, it is a subject you should study in its own right, given its importance. Below are a few concepts you should at least be aware of so that you can find out more about them. Where possible, try and *mirror and match* them in their speech patterns and body language (unless negative signals are being sent and it would be inappropriate).

Speed: Try and match the *speed* at which they speak and move.

Modality: Remember VAKOG. Visual, auditory, kinaesthetic, olfactory, gustatory. This is how they process information and it is evident in their language *"Does that feel right?", "Can you hear what I'm saying?", "Does that look right to you?", "Can you smell money here?"* Try and speak in their modality.

Body language: Again, this subject is so broad it can't be covered here, so I suggest you read up on it. Identifying gestures like nose-touching (potentially signifying a fib) to micro-signals like pupil dilation (potentially indicating desire) can be a useful way to decipher someone's state of mind. Basically, try and get people to - literally - open up. Uncross arms, use open gestures, use eye-contact. Lead the way and don't appear closed or defensive. You should be able to feel connection when you are in rapport with someone. You can certainly see it.

Anchoring, burn and relative numbers. There are pros and cons when it comes to who makes the first offer. The main advantage is that of setting the expectations. A disadvantage would be over-offering for something when they may have let you have it cheaper.

If you think something is worth paying, say, £100 for, then you could mention earlier in the conversation along the lines of "we'd typically pay in the range of £50 to £90 - or thereabouts, depending on circumstances". Setting a *range* (rather than a singular value) engenders negotiation rather than a simple yes/no. Setting the range lower than the perceived value sets the pace and when figures are hinted early on in discussions, the prices outlined will *burn* in the vendor's mind and *anchor* a useful reference point when making an offer later.

How many times have you watched a sales pitch where the vendor states something along the lines of "normally this [insert gadget here] would sell for [insert inflated price here] but that for [today only/this week only] they can have it for six easy payments of [insert highly contrasted and lower prices here]"?

The point is, without having set up expectations earlier by allowing an exaggerated price to *burn* for a while, there would be no contrast or perceived value when a different figure is presented later. Without reference points, any figures discussed are absolute and not relative.

If/when you do make a hard offer, try making it a *specific* value. It conveys the impression you've done your homework and have arrived at a carefully-calculated amount which gives the offer credibility and solidity.

As an aside, one technique used in property purchasing is 'round-number, round number, specific number'. For example (forget the actual values in this example as they are probably not relevant or appropriate, they're merely to demonstrate a principle), if the asking price for the property was £500k, you could initially offer (say) £420k which after discussions gets upped to £430k. After more discussions, this could then get upped to (say) £439,850. What does a being presented with a specific figure like that convey to you?

Remember, in general, if it's a distressed business you're likely looking to offer deferred payments (i.e. nothing or very little up front) and only acquire the assets (i.e. not the shares and associated liabilities) whereas if it's a profitable business, you're hopefully still looking to offer deferred payments (ideally linked to the performance of the business, although it's much more likely you'd be expected to pay a large chunk 'up front') and acquire the business in its entirety, including share ownership.

Hybrid solutions may be available where (say) a third of the asking price is paid up-front (for a good, profitable business), a third is deferred (i.e. vendor financed at x%) and the remaining third is financed by a third party.

Whatever you've decided, you need to ensure that you have enough working capital in the business so that you can trade. It's no good buying a business for a great price if the vendor takes all your cash and then the business is under-capitalised.

By now, you should have enough information/feedback to have either made a 'soft offer' or moved away from the deal. Any 'soft-close' offers that you've made will be couched in terms such as *"in principle ..."* or *"subject to due diligence ..."*.

If the deal was rejected by the vendor, then at the very least *find out why*. Go back and renegotiate if necessary. Make sure you learn as much as you can from the experience.

If you've managed to gain some kind of mutual agreement, then you're ready to make things more concrete and start investing time and resources in rigorous due-diligence. One thing to consider is that everything is still very fragile and that the seller will likely be having second thoughts.

Avoid seller's remorse. The last thing that you want after successfully negotiating a deal is for the seller to feel bad afterwards and change their mind. This might be the case if they feel they should have negotiated better or that your negotiation skills got the better of them.

Congratulate them. Let them know you think they got a great deal and that their negotiation skills served them well. Remember, when everything is conducted in a spirit of 'win-win' rather than 'win-lose', there will be less reason for after-negotiation doubt and remorse.

Get commitment. Let them know that your due diligence process incurs a cost for you. Consider getting some kind of loosely written agreement that they agree to, even though it won't necessarily be legally binding at this stage. Their commitment will be psychological rather than contractual.

Note, when it comes to completing a fully-fledged contract, get it drafted by your team. Apart from anything else (such as ensuring there's no onerous terms for you), this will increase the overall speed of the deal and any 'default options' you want included will hopefully be met with less resistance. As an aside, if the expression "heads of terms" is ever used, change it to "heads of agreement" as it's more collaborative. It will loosely outline both parties' expectations in terms of finances, timescales and handover. It's essential this is drafted properly for you by an expert in their field.

Once you have made an offer that's been accepted (in principle), then you'll want to have an agreement from the seller that you can (ideally with exclusivity) have a period of (no less than) a month for your due-diligence process.

8
Due Diligence

Ideally, you'll review a number of businesses, for practice if nothing else. Learn how to read financial statements, even though you'll use a specialist accountant (part of your 'power-team') to review the financial statements and identify potential problems.

As an aside, let your professional advisers find challenges, not negotiate. If you can, pay them fixed fees, not by the hour. If possible, pay them a fee contingent on the deal going through successfully. Explain that even if this one doesn't go through, they can earn money from a future deal you'll instruct them for.

Feel free to ask the business owner to identify existing and potential problems. You may hear things you wouldn't have thought of.

This is where you're 'looking under the bonnet' rather than just 'kicking the tyres'. You'll have already walked around the premises to get a feel for how the business is run. Now it's time to delve deeper. It's important not to skimp here or feel pressured. The process will take time (unless you abort partway through) so ensure you agree a window of *no less than a month*, more if necessary. When you agree your timeframe, make sure the vendor knows that the clock doesn't start ticking until you are in receipt of all the information and documentation you've asked for. Make sure you've got the right experts lined to help you: legal and financial (at the barest minimum), together with any brokers and/or other independent experts (like a specialist valuer).

Whilst you want to verify everything that you've been told, it will help considerably when the vendor doesn't feel like you don't trust them. So, trust ... but verify. Again, it's why the earlier time spent developing rapport and was so important. Further to rapport, diplomacy and tact are now called for. Remember the point about inoculating the vendor. There will almost certainly be some issue(s) that the due diligence process throws up because essentially, as well as verifying facts, you're also *looking for problems*. And this very process can cause problems in and of itself.

Consider your legal people for a moment. Putting aside the cynical view that their primary motivation is to make money for themselves, their *primary purpose* is not to facilitate a deal but to protect their client (and by extension, protect themselves from being sued for negligence). Even with the best of intentions, things can (and do) go wrong in business dealings and the only certain way that they can guarantee to protect their client in any deal is if the deal does not go through in the first place.

Of course, if lawyers were used at the moment of a marriage-proposal, nobody would ever get married ... and consequently nobody would ever go through divorce. It's a horrid outlook and impractical in reality although as a metaphor, it can serve to remind us that our legal representatives, whilst trying to protect us, can stifle a deal, so judgement is needed as well as aforementioned diplomacy.

Your accountant is in a similar position. They have the unenviable task of trying to evaluate and untangle the bewildering array of financial representations within an unfamiliar business (that may have had poor record-keeping) which has likely had its accounts prepared in such a way as to pay as little tax as possible. Business are (typically) managed to minimise tax liabilities and not show cash-flow and it may be advantageous for both sets of accountants to have full dialogue with each other. Again, like solicitors, the primary job of the purchaser's accountant is to protect their client above all else, even at the expense of killing deals if necessary. Depending on the size of the business you are looking to acquire, the prepared accounts may be *unverified* (i.e. not externally audited).

Be sure to answer the fundamental question *"how much will this business pay me?"* by establishing what the current business owner(s) take out of the business: profits, wages, expenses, benefits-in-kind etc.

From all the copious notes you've made so far during your discussions, look for anything that struck you as odd at the time or that needed further investigation or validation. Everything you've written down as a statement is not valid until checked. To help organise yourself and work forwards to a plan along a timeline, it might help to break the process down into six main business department such as:

Legal: Company structure, shareholders, contracts, agreements, leases, insurances etc.

Financial: Book-keeping, financial accounts, management accounts etc.

Sales and Marketing.

Production: Operations, equipment, stock, storage etc.

Systems and Processes: Admin, IT and software, disaster-recovery, facilities management etc.

People: Customers, staff, suppliers, R & D, training and development, health and safety etc.

⇨ **Legal**

Establish the ownership structure (shares etc.) paying attention to any changes in ownership.

Ensure the company actually owns the assets discussed e.g., website, IP (patents, licences, trademarks, marketing (website/domain, imagery, copyright, other collateral), stock, land and property, equipment, cash, receivables, leases etc.

Check any leases and ensure they can be transferred. You may need to prove 'worthiness' to the owner of the lease.

Ditto for licences, insurances etc.

Establish there are no pending lawsuits!

Have there ever been any significant insurance premium changes?

Review contracts (existing and pending) with clients, staff, suppliers etc.

Common covenants: non-disclosure, non-compete and non-poaching agreements. For you, the vendor and their staff, agents etc. A 'force-majeure' clause can protect you from your liabilities in the event of an unexpected event (flood, terrorism etc.)

"Business as usual". You might require the seller to agree to work/consult with/for the business for a set period to show you the ropes and help with a handover and promise to maintain existing procedures (working-hours, levels of service etc.) whilst not making any new and unusual agreements with staff, suppliers or clients. Note, very often the owner will not stay the full term and this is usually by mutual consent at that stage. After a while, they typically don't want to be around ... and you don't want them to be around either!

⇨ **Financial**

Is there a business plan to review?

Are there written records for the accounts and book-keeping processes?

Are the accounting methods consistent or have they been changed?

Has the company been sold before - or attempted to be sold before?

Do any of the directors (or key employees) have any criminal convictions?

Has an auditor, accountant, company secretary or other director resigned or moved recently?

Review *all* bank statements, cheque books etc. and highlight any anomalies.

Review the *trend* of revenues, costs and profits (normalise and remove one-off or unusual income and expenses to ascertain trends)

Review the last few years tax returns.

Verify accounts payable/receivable and check debtor-days and probable amount of bad debt.

Verify (or create) a cash-flow statement for the next six months.

Management accounts (while bank accounts tell the 'truth', management accounts paint a broader picture and are more subject to interpretation ... but nonetheless worth reviewing) Check lines of credit and any undue amounts owed (both by the business and to it).

Establish any contingent liabilities.

Have loans been serviced properly ... are there any bad credit issues?

Has the tax office ever had to issue warnings?

⇨ **Sales and Marketing**

Review trade publications for industry overview.

Is there a marketing plan in place?

What marketing activity is happening and what are the results? Is there a proper sales function or is it just haphazard?

Become a mystery shopper of a salesperson (not the business owner) and 'pump' them for information. See how they operate and identify strengths and weaknesses in their delivery.

From some elementary research you can conduct about the importance of working to a marketing plan, you should now be clear about the main marketing KPIs so there's no point repeating it here. Many businesses won't have this information to hand because they're simply not run well, which can be an opportunity for you, although it will hamper your investigations.

In my experience, if a company has a 'sales department', it's often simply one person who is the default salesperson. One person is not an ideal number because it doesn't create any competition and it's difficult to gauge the output of a single individual. It can be the sign of sick sales but it can be improved and could therefore represent a potential opportunity.

⇨ Production

Are there written records for the production processes?

What's the quality control/feedback process?

See if any capital equipment has to be replaced soon, this could be expensive. Check leases.

Get a manifest of stock, understand how it's been valued and consider its obsolescence.

Check for loans against assets.

What are the maintenance contracts in place for software and equipment?

What is the supply chain?

What key materials or resources required?

What are the handling/disposal requirements for unused/unwanted/spent/discarded materials/wastage etc. (e.g., sensitive documents, obsolete equipment etc.)

⇨ Systems and Processes

Are there written records for the systems and processes, e.g. admin? How are bills paid?

How are payments made?

What's the state of the buildings and situation with rents, leases, expiry dates etc?

What software is in place? Is it custom or off the shelf? Who maintains it?

What security and backup systems are in place? Where is data stored? Who has access?

Who has keys for the building?

What's the process in the event of a disaster? (Fire, flood, hack etc.) Review the risk management policy and business continuity plan.

What's the accident rate? Is there a proper health and safety policy?

What certifications, licences, regulatory bodies are required/maintained?

⇨ **People**

What other activities/businesses are the owner(s) involved in?

Have they ever been bankrupt? What's their credit rating?

Any conflicts of interests for the directors, managers, staff or suppliers?

Is there an organisational chart?

Who are the key people and how difficult would it be to replace them if they left?

Check employment terms such as salary, overtime, bonuses, profit-sharing, pay-rises, holidays, sickness, pensions, redundancy, termination etc.

What are the recruitment policies?

Is there a written code of conduct?

Have CVs been checked?

Any known issues such as health, financial, litigation, personal issues etc.?

What's the rate of staff turnover?

What/how are professional qualifications required/maintained?

What/how are memberships, professional bodies, certifications etc. required/maintained?

Which staff have proved problematic or had disciplinaries?

What's the morale of the staff? Do they get along?

Are there instances of harassment, bullying, discrimination or other antisocial issues?

Are any staff capable of taking key contracts to a competitor or setting up for themselves?

Who are the key customers? Do any represent a significant threat if they go elsewhere?

What are the terms of their contracts?

What's the breakdown of customers vs. margin?

How long have key customers been in place and how were they acquired?

Get a short-list of clients lost (and reasons) over the last couple of years.

Do any clients need undue time, servicing or are unprofitable due to other issues?

How profitable are any clients who appear to be unhappy?

Are any major contracts due for renewal?

Is there a history of complaints from any customers?

Who are the key suppliers?

Do any suppliers have any undue influence?

Are any major supplier contracts about to expire or be renegotiated?

You can see from these examples (which are numerous but by no means exhaustive) that you'll need to ask around. Ask people other than the business owner. Speak to staff. Establish (without causing any concerns) what they think of the company. What do the clients think of it? What do the suppliers think?

It cannot be overstated that your legal and financial people need to go through their various processes before you proceed any further.

9
Funding

If you've structured the deal so that there's a payment up front, then you'll need to find money. Of course, you can decide to simply use your own money (that you've earned, saved, inherited etc.) but then you'll be limited by what you have. Sooner or later, it always runs out. Most people restrict their own possibilities by limiting their thinking to just the capital they personally have direct access to. However, for those people that get good at securing finance from other sources, potential funds are *unlimited*. Stop, think. That's another game-changing concept, right there:

"The number and size of businesses you acquire isn't limited by how much money you have, rather by how well you structure deals and secure investment."

There are a number of potential sources of finance. Assuming it's not simply a gift or a loan from a trusting friend or family member, the person providing it will want to see some kind of *return on investment* and/or ensure they have some degree of assurance that they'll have their money back. To this end, you can offer to guarantee their money by providing security in an asset that they can control if you default on the payment(s). Again, most people considering getting business finance simply think in terms of bank loans, yet the possibilities of how capital is borrowed/repaid and from whom are endless. The main variables to consider when acquiring capital are:

- Source of funding

- RoI

- Repayment structure : Types and Term

- Security/Guarantee

Some Potential Sources of Finance

- *Banks* - Overdrafts secured/unsecured loans: personal loans and commercial, credit cards(!).

- *Specialist business lenders.*

- *Crowdfunding websites* - peer to peer investors e.g. Funding circle (UK).

- *Sales of shares* - investors/angels.

- *Invoice factoring.*

- *Supplier/customer/staff financing.*

- *Other business owners.*

- *Personal finance*: draw from (or borrow against) retirement funds/life insurance funds.

- *Government loans*/grants - SBA Loans (US).

- *Vendor finance.*

- *Family/friends/colleagues/others.*

Remember, selling shares is the most expensive form of financing in the long run although bringing in an 'angel' or another investor with experience does mean that, as well as cash, you may well negotiate access to their expertise and other resources.

Whilst most of those suggestions listed above are relatively obvious and can easily be investigated (e.g. getting a loan from a bank, crowdfunding website or a specialist business lender) there are definitely occasions when it can pay to be creative and spend a bit of time looking at other possibilities.

Certainly, if there are any grants, subsidies or loans available, it'd be a sin not to use them.

Also, is it possible that some common denominators may want to join together to help finance the business? For example, if a particular company is servicing some clients and they don't want to see the business stop trading (if it's in difficulties), perhaps they can form a cooperative and help you finance the acquisition of the business in return for part equity and/or financial returns. A similar arrangement can apply for suppliers or staff.

The two main alternative sources of finance that I'd like to spend a little time considering is *vendor financing* and *non-professional investors*.

Vendor Financing

Getting the owner of the business to sell you their business and *pay for the finance of it* has to be some kind of magic, doesn't it? But it's not as crazy as it sounds. As we've already covered, they may have very compelling reasons to get out of their business (some of which may be a concern for you, others an opportunity). The main benefits to the vendor (which you may want to remember during your negotiations) are:

- More potential buyers (especially if the banks are not forthcoming).
- Potential to keep any interest the banks would have charged.
- Potential to increase overall price (due to more potential buyers).
- Speed.
- Less limitations/hurdles to jump through.
- Easier/more flexible for negotiations.
- Potential tax benefits.
- A future income stream, potentially 'residual income'.
- Gives the vendor some degree of control/leverage over the transaction.

Unlike a bank, they know their business - they *believe* in the business.

The main benefit for you is that they have 'skin in the game' and are committed to everything working because their loan-repayments from you are contingent upon your success with the company performance meeting pre-arranged criteria ... with no nasty 'surprises'.

Non-professional investors

In recent years, the banks have been paying very low interest rates and so people who have kept their savings in a bank are often getting very poor returns on them. After inflation, they're probably actually losing money in real terms. That hurts.

You can offer them *significantly* better returns. Plus, you can negotiate. It's a lot easier to spin ideas around with your friend/brother/sister/father-in law than you ever can with a bank!

People with money to invest are everywhere. There are a lot more people around that have savings squirreled away than there are banks. If you can grow and maintain a 'sales pipeline' of private investors that can provide funds for your businesses, properties and other financial projects that pay an attractive return then you're in a position to earn much higher revenues at a vastly accelerated rate. For this reason, make a plan to start attracting investors for now and the future.

Ask what they want. Uncover their hopes/fears/desires etc. Use everything you learned in previous sections about selling and negotiation. Be flexible and creative.

Some points to bear in mind when looking for non-professional-investor finance:

- The law. Familiarise yourself with the law regarding soliciting money and borrowing it e.g. Financial Conduct Authority (FCA) legislation PS13/3 (in the UK).

- Mindset. Become an opportunity to help people make good returns. You're not 'begging for money', so act accordingly! Don't be a 'spiv' or too 'British'.

- Pipeline. You'll need to build credibility with a pipeline of potential investors over time. Business / social networking etc. People with money are everywhere (often with people that look as though they don't have it) from savings, pensions, inheritances, redundancies, winnings, insurances, endowments etc.

- It's not just who you know, it's who they know. Remember the expression your network is your net-worth. 200 people that know another 200 people is 40,000 people. Always ask if they know someone that might be interested in investing ...

- Ideally, have more than one investor available so that if you need money quickly, or one investor pulls out, you're not isolated.

- Don't offer deals as 'too good to be true'. Non-professional investors are likely expecting very pedestrian rates of return and they will want their money secured in an easy-to-understand way.

- Gain credibility. Highlight success of your existing business and/or previous deals. Get noticed. Have testimonials and social proof. Drip feed information to your 'pipeline', via social networks, newsletters, meetups etc.

- Advertise occasional deals. Rather than waiting until 'that one deal' arrives, you can announce other deals occasionally (even if you're not intending to proceed with them) and see which people are interested, then offer to keep them on the shortlist for next time.

Some Repayment Possibilities

Once again, you have the opportunity to be creative in how you repay any capital that you've been provided with.

- Flat Fee. Pay the principle + interest (lump-sum) after agreed period.

- Repayments. Receive principle + interest (monthly payments) for agreed no. of payments.

- Interest Only. Pay interest-only (monthly payments) for an agreed period (with a 'balloon payment' at the end) which can be extended/renegotiated.

- Share of profits/revenue. E.g., shares of monthly profits/revenue or annual dividends.

- Hybrid. E.g., monthly repayments plus a profit share mix.

- Payments in kind.

How about that last one? I.e., providing goods/services paid from the company (or suppliers) at preferential rates to the provider of capital.

Security for The Lender(s)

If you have assets in the target business, *getting finance against it* should be significantly easier. Otherwise, you will probably be expected to offer some kind of business guarantee or personal guarantee against other assets that either you own or have control over.

Again, being creative, they don't always have to be your own assets or your own guarantee. Think for a moment about how many parents provide a third-party rent-guarantee to help their children get a rental accommodation.

Here are some other sources of security you (or others) can leverage against:

Business assets. Property, stock, plant/equipment, vehicles, contracts, purchase orders, accounts receivable, people (football players have been used as collateral!), animals (racehorses have been used), licences/rights/permissions etc.

Personal assets. Land, property (via a second mortgage, first/ second charges), cars, boats, investments, savings-secured loans, insurance policies, future income (paychecks/insurances/ endowments etc.) Again, you can be creative, particularly if dealing with individuals rather than banks.

Demonstrate You Mean Business

If you are looking to get finance from a bank or other financial institution, you'll need to *work with them*. Remember, ultimately they want to lend money, even if it doesn't feel like it. Be prepared to jump through their hoops. Make the loan officer's job easier for them. Communicate well and give them access to all the documentation they request. Get them on your side and build relationships. Allow plenty of time.

As well as credit checking, past performance/repayments are a factor. Consider whether (as part of your long-term goals) whether it's worth buying something on credit through them – (even a small business) for practice and to build up your 'past performance' track record.

You can expect that banks (and also savvy private investors), are likely to want to see a business plan too, as well as your track record, and evidence of collateral. Putting together a business plan can help give *you* clarity as well, so it's a worthwhile exercise.

As this is primarily designed to create confidence in a lender that you will be able to flourish and therefore meet repayments, I have added sub-sections in key areas, namely "Opportunities for improvement" which you can complete.

Typical Business Plan

Executive summary

- Business concept
- Overview
- Current position
- Historic achievements

Product/service summary

Financial Summary

- Overview of finances
- Funding required

Vision statement

- Mission statement

Market opportunity

Objectives and Goals

Opportunities for improvement

Company description

- Comprehensive, descriptive account of the business and related factors

Opportunities for improvement

Market/industry analysis

Industry

- Innovation/disruption
- PEST issues: Political, environmental, societal, technological
- Trends

Market

- Size
- Share
- Target market
- Target market needs

Competition

- Barriers to entry/growth
- Direct competition

- Indirect competition
- Your competitive advantage(s)
- Company positioning
- USPs

  Opportunities for improvement

Products and Services

- How the products / services work
- How they're delivered
- Lifecycles
- Costs/margins
    - Products/service development
- Research
- Training

  Opportunities for improvement

Organisation

- Directors
- Management team
  (Identify any gaps and how they will be filled)
- Production staff

(Identify any gaps and how they will be filled)

- Operating Model
- Logistics

Opportunities for improvement

Sales and marketing strategy

- Products
- Pricing
- Promotion (and place)
  - Communications strategy
  - Distribution channels
- Customer acquisition
- Sales strategy

Opportunities for improvement

Financial Summary

- Revenue model
  - Income streams
- Expected incomes, assets, expenses, liabilities, profits
- Sensitivity analysis
- Cash-flow projections

Opportunities for improvement

Funding

- Amount(s) required and when (i.e., which stages
- Breakdown of how funding will be allocated/spent
- Exit strategy: timeline, expected financial outcome
- Potential buyers:
    - Profile of general potential buyers
    - Reasons why they would be interested to buy
    - List of specific potential buyers

Appendices

- Supporting documentation
    - income statement, balance sheet, cash-flow statement
    - Awards, patents, certificates, key contracts won
- Contingencies
    - SWOT - strengths, weaknesses, opportunities, threats
    - Alternative strategies for sales and marketing

- Known issues and how they can be mitigated

- Disaster plan summary

A last note about getting finance - if you're getting it from a bank or other financial institution, expect to wait a few weeks from (their) receipt of documentation. Furthermore, a share purchase will likely take even longer than just acquiring the assets.

10
Buy and Fix it!

If the due-diligence process has highlighted irreconcilable problems - or you simply don't feel right about the deal at this point (try and differentiate between simple nerves and a more sinister 'gut feeling' that something's not right) then obviously, you won't proceed.

If the due-diligence has shown that the deal would have been viable but the numbers weren't as good as you'd originally anticipated, then you can show your findings to the existing owner and see if it can be renegotiated so that it can be made to work for you. Can you work with the seller? If not, the numbers may be meaningless.

If you've got this far (and the due diligence was okay) i.e. you've negotiated, agreed a price and terms and you have the finance arranged (or can get it) then you're now in a position to go ahead ... woohoo!

Signing papers (ensuring everyone is present that needs to sign), transferring titles etc. is obviously best left to the lawyers. However, it won't be them that's responsible for making the business turn a profit though, so you'll need to refer back to the section outlining different ways you can add value to a business and/or cut costs from it and have an *action plan* to implement this.

Immediate Things to Do

- Do the deal-signing early for any last-minute changes while everyone is still available.

- Sign the contracts, after any amendments.

- Ensure title(s) to all assets have been transferred and check stock if appropriate.

- Change passwords for key areas e.g., CRM, ERP, bank accounts, email accounts etc.

- Get the paperwork ready to prove you now own the company to staff, banks, suppliers, customers etc.

- Make sure the bank accepts you as the new owner ASAP.

- Request new credit card numbers and cancel old ones.

- Announce the news to key people (see below).

No matter how smoothly you transition everything and how well you market and manage your newly acquired business, there will be general disruption and fear which you'll need to try and mitigate.

Confidence, Operations and Revenue

The first quarter is the hardest and it's essential to maintain *confidence* throughout the business, manage the change of *operations* and ensure *revenue* doesn't drop. Some people say that you can expect revenue to drop for the first 6 months (and perhaps you can take consolation from that if it happens), however, this certainly doesn't mean you should take it as a hard and fast rule fact and indeed I'd avoid accepting it as a norm instead *aim to increase revenue*.

Confidence is all about communications. Remember (from section one of this book) your market(s), message(s) and media. The 'markets' will be staff, clients, suppliers, other stakeholders ... including the previous owner (see below).

Message(s): Staff

Firstly, they might not even know anything about the change of ownership, depending on how the transfer process was conducted. Have something prepared to communicate to them. If they already know there's been a transfer of ownership, you'll need to reassure them (if they're staying) or let them go if they're not. Meet with top management first to give them your good news (or bad news) accordingly. They'll need to understand how the transition is being implemented and what they're expected to do with themselves and people under their charge. This is the time to share your vision and expectations.

Later (after you've made a general announcement to the rest of the business), you'll need to meet with management again to assign (or confirm) goals, responsibilities, boundaries and so on. You'll set the at this point tone (won't get a second chance to make a first impression) and confirm job descriptions for everyone in the organisational chart. Including your own!

Message(s): Customers

Tip: Imagine your customers as your boss - what would they ask you to do?

Interview them, find out what they want. Let them know you want to give them great value.

What's your new pricing strategy? (This communicates your positioning).

Go back to old customers and tell them it's under new management.

Message(s): Suppliers

For the outside world, you can run a press release, ensuring you frame everything in the positive, after all ... it's good news!

Apart from your staff and clients, your suppliers will want reassurance, especially the ones where the business has run a credit balance. You have different options here.

You can reassure them that you're the 'good guy' and that their credit with you is safe and they should continue doing business with you. If the business was stressed, you can request a payment 'holiday' or better terms.

For those other suppliers where you don't owe them anything of any significance, it's an opportunity for them to prove themselves to you.

As this text is largely geared towards small business owners that already own a business, there will probably be some duplication at this point in terms of provision of supplies and/or services (deduplication is one of the ways wwyou can make the acquired business more efficient), meaning that the supplier allowed to remain should be based on merit. However, this doesn't take into account any social capital you've invested in your incumbent supplier and there is a case for keeping diversity of suppliers.

Nonetheless, this can be an ideal time to create a little competition between suppliers or at the very least, revisit agreements you've already got in place and see if you can negotiate better terms.

If the previous owner is still working in the business, either as a temporary consultant or as a long term employee, then technically they'll be a supplier now as well. You'll likely need to treat them with kid gloves and, depending on how they're coping, you may need to give them some slack, after all they are used to being an entrepreneur, not an employee.

It's very possible you may need to politely (but firmly) set boundaries to their authority. They may even be experiencing seller's remorse and the environment or your relationship with them can become awkward if not handled carefully. As already mentioned, for one reason or another, they often don't stay around very long.

Now, Fix the Business!

Review the section earlier about how to add value and/or cut costs. List out what you need to do and prioritise it in some kind of action-plan. Use good old 80/20 thinking and *prioritise*.

Quick Ways of Cutting Expenditure

- Review *all expenditure.*

- Review all monies going out of the bank account(s) (especially direct debits and other automated payments).

- Review/restrict who has authority for payments and purchasing.

- Reduce headcount (if practical).

- Deduplicate suppliers.

- Get better terms from suppliers and/or shop around.

- Leverage goodwill from suppliers e.g. get free rent for a few months.

- Extend creditor days.

- Sell - or rent out - assets that aren't being used effectively.

- Implement organisational efficiencies.

Quick Ways of Increasing Revenue

- Get cash in from customers/debtors.

- Remove admin delays so all invoices are sent out immediately.

- Increase prices.

- Leverage all your acquired (and existing) clients to up-sell/down-sell/cross-sell.

- Have a special event to promote sales.

- Contact lost clients.

- Energise the sales department. Give ambitious targets and contingent bonuses.

- Ramp up marketing, starting with no-cost/low cost methods e.g. joint-venturing/referrals.

Rinse and Repeat!

If you made it this far and survived, why not strive to have a portfolio of several businesses? With synergy, the value you derive from the whole is more than the sum of the parts. Each business can complement and strengthen the others. Alternatively, consider consolidating several businesses into one and streamlining them all for super efficiency.

Perhaps a combination of diversification and consolidation would be best. The sky's the limit! Depending on your personality, you might find it more fun than 'working'.

If everything has gone to plan, you'll have acquired a business, increased its value and can now sell it (flip) for significantly more than you bought it for or enjoy the ongoing profits.

Congratulations!

Recap

Hopefully, you should have picked up these main points from section two:

- Company growth (i.e. your wealth) by acquisition is quicker than organic growth.

- Lots of people will sell their businesses, if approached.

- You don't have to buy the risk, you can just buy the assets.

- You can buy now, pay later.

- You're not limited by your own money - capital is everywhere.

- Develop your power-team (legal, financial, broker etc.)

- Have multiple options - build pipelines of deals and funds.

- Be vigilant - things can and do go wrong. Get good at due diligence.

- Practice 'dummy deals' to build up confidence and experience.

- Add value and/or cut costs to maximise profits.

- Rinse, repeat to build up your portfolio.

***

Thank You

That's it, onwards and upwards. I hope to have provided at least a few nuggets that you can use for your business journey. So, if you've had some value, please tell others. If not, keep quiet ... but tell me!

Should you want to get in touch, there's a contact form at:

www.michaelknight.co.uk

Good luck!

About the Author

Mike Knight has worn lots of (business) hats since finally incorporating his own company in 1998.

After several years providing web development and online marketing services, he spent a while in Australia before he and his family returned to the UK where his sons are now rapidly growing up. In 2015, Mike's company pivoted (yet again) and decided to concentrate efforts within the business to business arena, specifically servicing the growing IT industry.

Further to working with hundreds of UK businesses, with an MBA from The University of Gloucestershire and having been made a fellow of the Chartered Institute of Marketing, Mike Knight (MBA FCIM) has helped various businesses and individuals buy, sell and merge companies so he is now in a position to share some of that knowledge in this simple-to-read guide aimed at helping small business owners enjoy the benefits of acquisition whilst hopefully avoiding the pitfalls.